IN THE DAYS OF THE
VAQUEROS

AMERICA'S FIRST TRUE COWBOYS

◆◆◆

BY RUSSELL FREEDMAN

CLARION BOOKS

NEW YORK

CLARION BOOKS
a Houghton Mifflin Company imprint
215 Park Avenue South, New York, NY 10003
Text copyright © 2001 by Russell Freedman

Book design by Sylvia Frezzolini Severance.
The text was set in 13-point Stempel Garamond.

www.houghtonmifflinbooks.com

Printed in Singapore.

Frontispiece: In this 1849 painting by Augusto Ferran,
three California vaqueros, two on horseback and one on foot,
lasso a runaway steer along a rough road.

Library of Congress Cataloging-in-Publication Data

Freedman, Russell.
In the days of the vaqueros : America's first true cowboys / by Russell Freedman.
p.   cm.
Includes bibliographical references (p. 61).
ISBN 0-395-96788-0
1. Mexican American cowboys—Southwest, New—History—Juvenile literature.
2. Ranch life—Southwest, New—History—Juvenile literature. 3. Frontier and pioneer life—
Southwest, New—Juvenile literature. 4. Southwest, New—Social life and customs—Juvenile literature.
5. Southwest, New—History—Juvenile literature. [1. Cowboys. 2. Mexico—Social life and customs.
3. Southwest, New—Social life and customs. 4. Frontier and pioneer life—Mexico. 5. Frontier and
pioneer life—Southwest, New.] I. Title.

F790.M5F74 2001
636.2'13'09236872073—dc21   2001017357

TWP   10 9 8 7 6 5 4 3 2 1

For Isaac Ambrosio

◆◆◆◆◆◆◆◆◆◆◆◆◆◆◆◆◆◆◆◆◆◆

CONTENTS

From Wild Scenes in South America, *Ramón Paez, New York, 1862.*

◆◆

This is the ballad of the white horse
That happily took off one Sunday,
Heading north. . . .

His bold rider removed the reins.
He removed the saddle and rode bareback.
Like lightning he galloped across the plains
Between green hills and the sky.

—From "El Caballo Blanco,"
a Mexican ballad

Hunting Wild Horses. *Painting by William T. Ranney, 1846.*

◆◆◆◆◆◆◆◆◆◆◆◆◆◆◆◆◆◆◆◆◆◆◆◆◆◆◆◆◆

CHAPTER ONE

THE FIRST OF THEIR KIND

Long ago—before cattle came to Texas, before George Washington crossed the Delaware, before the Pilgrims landed at Plymouth Rock—cowboys rode the range in Spanish Mexico. They called themselves *vaqueros,* or cowherders, from *vaca,* the Spanish word for cow.

Vaqueros were herding cattle on the Mexican plains nearly five hundred years ago. Often they rode barefoot. They wore what clothes they had at hand. In the eyes of their Spanish masters, they were nothing more than poor Indian laborers on horseback. But they were the first of their kind, and they invented the cowboy trade as we know it today.

The beginnings of the cowboy trade can be traced back to the time of Christopher Columbus, who introduced cattle to North America and re-introduced the horse. Wild horses once roamed the grasslands of the Americas, but they disappeared mysteriously thousands of years before the first European explorers arrived. Columbus reported after his voyage in 1492 that he had found no horses or cattle in the New World.

On Columbus's second voyage, his fleet of seventeen ships carried 1,200 Spanish settlers and as many horses and cattle as the little vessels could hold. On January 2, 1494, the fleet dropped anchor off the coast of Hispaniola, the island in the Caribbean now shared by Haiti and the Dominican Republic. The crew lowered the gangplanks and unloaded the livestock that had survived the long ocean journey—twenty-four stallions, ten mares, and an unknown number of cattle.

More horses and cattle were brought to the Americas as Spanish colonists settled in present-day Puerto Rico, Cuba, Jamaica, and other islands of the West Indies. From the islands, livestock soon spread to the Mexican mainland, where Hernán Cortés and his band of *conquistadores* had overwhelmed Tenochtitlan, the capital of the Aztecs, captured the Aztec emperor Moctezuma, and claimed all of Aztec Mexico for Spain.

Mexico's wide-open spaces were ideal for raising livestock, and during the 1500s colonists arrived with increasing numbers of horses and cattle. Back home in Spain, the animals were kept penned up in pastures. But in Mexico, they were allowed to wander at will, finding their own grass and water. Many of them escaped to run free, creating enormous herds of wild horses and cattle. They roamed far and wide through the valleys and plains from Vera Cruz to Mexico City like gigantic carpets moving across the countryside. "You cannot exaggerate their numbers or imagine the spectacle before your eyes," a Spanish visitor reported.

Soon cattle ranches began to appear throughout Spanish Mexico. The earliest ranches were started by Cortés's conquistadores, soldiers who came to the New World in search of gold, and by Roman Catholic missionaries, who came in search of souls to save.

The conquistadores had helped Cortés conquer Aztec Mexico, and they wanted to be compensated for their services to the Spanish crown. They

Moctezuma II, Emperor of Aztec Mexico at the time of the Spanish conquest. Seized as a hostage by Hernán Cortés, Moctezuma was killed when the Aztecs rose against the Spanish invaders.

The central area of Tenochtitlan, capital of the Aztec empire (a reconstruction). The city was destroyed in 1521 after a three-month siege.

Hernán Cortés, Spanish conquistador and the conqueror of Mexico. Cortés became the richest man in the New World. Drawing by José Cisneros.

were rewarded with *encomiendas,* huge sprawling estates that included all the Indian towns and villages within their boundaries. Cortés himself received an encomienda that embraced twenty-two settlements inhabited by more than twenty-three thousand Indians.

The holder of an encomienda, who was known as the *encomendero,* ruled like an all-powerful feudal lord. He was responsible for protecting the Indians in his domain and making sure that they were instructed in the Christian faith. The Indians, in turn, were required to provide labor. They had to work for the encomendero without pay. Like slaves, they had no choice. If an Indian laborer tried to run away, Spanish soldiers were sent with bloodhounds to hunt him down. When caught, he was whipped.

An encomendero ruled his domain like an all-powerful feudal lord. He was entitled to the labor of all Indians living on his land. Drawing by José Cisneros.

Encomiendas also were awarded to the Spanish *padres*, the priests who founded Roman Catholic missions in Mexico. The padres taught their Indian charges Spanish values and Christian doctrine. They administered justice and punished those who rebelled. Their converts built churches and schools, tended orchards, planted crops, and worked as servants. Eventually they herded cattle for the mission fathers.

Because the cattle ran wild, wandering off in all directions, mingling with animals from neighboring ranches, it became necessary to round them up once or twice a year. Then they could be counted and sorted. New calves could be branded with their owners' marks and some animals slaughtered for their hides, fat, and meat.

Spanish landed gentlemen looked down their noses at such hard, dirty, sweaty work. They rode horses proudly and with style, sitting tall and erect in their velvet-covered saddles, but they never soiled their hands with manual labor. They considered it beneath their dignity to actually work cattle. The mission fathers, many of them the sons of Spanish nobility, often felt the same way.

The only ranch hands available were the Indian laborers, who did all the work at Spanish missions and at the big landed estates. There was just one problem: Indians were forbidden by law, on penalty of death, to ride horses, which were considered weapons of war.

But the mission fathers were laws unto themselves, and they needed help. They were the first to solve the problem. Ignoring the Spanish colonial authorities in faraway Mexico City, they taught their Indian converts to ride, equipped them with lances and knives, and sent them out to hunt for cattle.

That's when the vaquero, the original cowboy, was born. From the beginning, he was a spectacular horseman—as he had to be to handle wild herds on the open range. In time, he developed the tools and skills that he would pass along to cowboys everywhere.

During these years, the Indians of Mexico and other parts of New Spain were granted certain rights. By the 1660s, the encomiendas with their system of forced labor were being phased out. No longer pressed into service as an unpaid worker, the vaquero became a hired ranch hand earning a small monthly wage. By now, many of the vaqueros were *mestizos,* men of mixed Indian and Spanish parentage. Others were free blacks, descendants of slaves who had been brought from Africa by way of Spain.

The great cattle ranches, meanwhile, remained in the hands of the wealthy Spanish colonists and the mission fathers. Ranches were spreading throughout the region. Missionaries and colonists introduced cattle to Mexico's rugged northern provinces, then to the wild frontier regions of New Spain—present-day Texas, Arizona, and New Mexico—and finally, during the late 1700s, to the warm grassy valleys of Spanish California. And wherever the cattle went, they were accompanied by skilled vaqueros.

The same thing was happening on grasslands throughout the Americas, wherever cattle could be raised. The Mexican vaquero had South American counterparts in the Argentine *gaucho,* the Brazilian *vaquerio,* the Chilean *huaso,* and the Venezuelan and Colombian *llanero.*

In Argentina, and later in the United States, the cowboy became known as a romantic figure, a national hero on horseback. But in Mexico, the vaquero was never idealized in this manner. When Mexicans celebrated a horseman, it was usually the *charro,* the aristocratic gentleman rider, who received all the attention.

The charro was a landowner, a person of wealth and prestige. The vaquero remained for hundreds of years a poorly paid laborer. He was a landless *peón,* a man at the bottom of the social ladder, often illiterate, usually in debt to his employer, largely ignored by artists and writers, and little noticed by his fellow countrymen.

An Indian mission vaquero.
Drawing by José Cisneros.

Artist James Walker's impression of a cattle drive, ca. 1877.

CHAPTER TWO

RODEO

Cattle roundups on the open range began in Mexico during the 1520s and continued for the next four hundred years. They were called *rodeos*, from the Spanish word *rodear*, which means "to go around" or "to surround or encircle." And that's exactly what happened to the free-roaming, far-ranging, fast-running cattle.

Vaqueros from neighboring ranches sometimes joined together in a rodeo. Each ranch sent a team of riders, who often came from a great distance. A really big roundup might cover hundreds of square miles, last for weeks, and involve three or four hundred vaqueros along with tens of thousands of head of cattle.

The men rode onto the plains and fanned out. They flushed cattle from their hiding places in thickets, gulleys, and ravines and sent them trotting across the countryside toward a central roundup ground.

Bawling and bellowing, animals began to bunch together, forming a great milling herd as the circle of horsemen tightened around them. Finally, their wild instincts flaring, the cattle kicked up their heels and broke into a frenzied headlong stampede.

Bulls, their eyes red with rage, charged straight ahead with lowered horns. Calves leaped into the air, legs stiff and tails erect. Vaqueros galloped back and forth, dodging in and out through clouds of swirling dust, yelling and whistling, cracking whips, waving *sarapes.* At times, cattle and horses

In a Stampede.
Drawing by
Frederic Remington, 1888.

collided, sending riders tumbling to the ground and, if they were lucky, scrambling to safety. "A man can't die until his time comes," the vaqueros always said.

At the roundup ground, the cattle gradually calmed down and started to graze. Then the mounted riders began to sort the animals according to owner, marking each new calf with its mother's brand.

In the early days, during the 1500s, vaqueros used *garrochas,* long iron-tipped lances, to poke and prod the cattle as they separated them and checked their brands. A calf singled out for branding was taken from its

In the early days, cowboys throughout Latin America used garrochas, long iron-tipped lances, as tools to work cattle. This watercolor by an unknown nineteenth-century artist shows a Colombian llanero in action.

mother and prodded toward an open fire, where branding irons were being heated. Men on foot wrestled the little animal to the ground and pinned it down. One of them grabbed the iron, heated until it was cherry red, then pressed it home, burning the ranch's special mark into the calf's hairy flank.

Another vaquero used a sharpened knife to cut a notch in the calf's ear. The shape and position of the notch was an additional way of identifying the animal. When the calf was released, it struggled to its feet and shook its head, splattering blood. Then it ran off, bawling loudly and searching for its mother.

A steer marked for slaughter was brought down with an instrument called a *desjarretadera,* or hocking knife—a curved steel blade attached to the end of a stout pole ten or twelve feet long. Holding the pole in his right hand with the knife blade aimed forward, a vaquero galloped after the running steer. Closing in on the animal, he thrust the pole ahead of his horse. The razor-sharp edge of the knife sliced into the steer's hind leg, cutting the tendon and sending the helpless animal crashing to the ground. This is called hamstringing.

The vaquero then leaped off his horse, pulled out his hand knife, and plunged it into the steer's neck, just behind the horns, severing the spinal cord and killing the animal instantly.

Hamstringing was swift and sure, but deadly. An animal brought down in this way was crippled and always had to be killed. During the 1550s, when cattle became more valuable for their hides than for their flesh, vast numbers of animals were killed in this manner—much as buffalo would be slaughtered for their hides three centuries later on the American Great Plains.

Mexican ranchers slaughtered so many thousands of cattle that the Spanish authorities became alarmed. They feared that the herds might never recover. In 1574, the hamstringing of cattle was outlawed and the hocking knife banned. Anyone found to be using a hocking knife was fined twenty pesos (more than many men could pay) or was whipped in public. The penalty was one hundred lashes.

In place of the hocking knife, vaqueros turned to a new tool, *la reata,* the lariat, a braided rawhide rope with a slipknot, or running noose, at one end. This was also called a *lazo,* or lasso. It allowed a horseman to catch a steer and hold it for branding or some other purpose without causing serious injury.

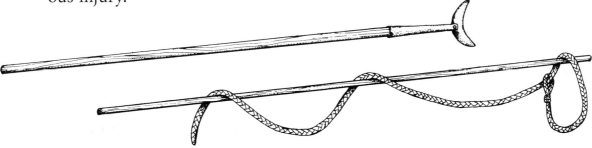

Top: A desjarretadera, or hocking knife, used to cripple a running steer.
Bottom: An early version of the lariat.

At first, the lariat wasn't thrown. Instead, the noose was placed at the tip of a long pole. Racing after a steer, a vaquero lowered the end of his pole and slipped the noose over the steer's horns. Then he pulled back to tighten the noose. The other end of the rope was tied to the cinch on his saddle, or sometimes to his horse's tail.

Eventually, the vaquero became an expert at twirling a lariat above his head, then throwing the noose to snare a steer on the run. Depending on the task at hand, the noose could be thrown crossways, from the left, from the right, underhand, overhand, or backward.

The *mangana,* from the Spanish word *mano* for "hand" or "forefoot," was an overhand throw that opened the noose to catch the animal's front legs as it stepped forward. The *piale,* from *pie,* for "foot," was an under-

Vaqueros were experts at twirling lariats above their heads.

hand toss that caught the animal's hind legs. Other throws could catch a running steer's horns or head. With a properly thrown lariat, a scrawny 130-pound vaquero could bring down a massive 1,000-pound steer.

The vaquero now began to tie his end of the lariat to his saddle horn, instead of to the saddle's cinch or his horse's tail. Once he had roped a steer, he took several quick turns of the lariat around the horn, letting the rope slide along to gain some leverage before bringing the animal to a stop. But he had to work fast. A thumb caught between the whizzing rope and the horn could be amputated when the steer pulled the rope taut.

Snubbing the rope around the saddle horn to hold a steer tight was called *dar la vuelta,* "to make the turn." The same technique, used thousands of

Snubbing the rope around the saddle horn.

times over hundreds of years, came to be called, simply, "dally" by American cowboys.

While he relied on his lariat, a skilled vaquero could also bring down a running steer with his bare hands. He would ride up behind the animal, grab its tail, twist the steer off balance, and send it tumbling horn over heel through the dust.

The lariat, or lasso, became the single most important tool for handling cattle on the open range.

Vaqueros in a courtyard. Painting by Edward Borein, ca. 1925.

♦♦♦♦♦♦♦♦♦♦♦♦♦♦♦♦♦♦♦♦♦♦♦♦♦

CHAPTER THREE

HACIENDAS AND *RANCHOS*

By the 1700s, most Mexican vaqueros lived and worked on gigantic cattle-raising *haciendas,* estates so vast that it might take two weeks or more simply to ride around one. The great size of the haciendas was matched by the power of their owners.

The center of a hacienda was like a small town, with the main buildings grouped around a square. The biggest building was the *casa grande,* home of the *hacendado,* the owner of the estate. He lived in a palatial mansion with oil paintings on the walls and bearskin rugs on the tiled floors. As master and self-appointed authority of his isolated community, the hacendado settled disputes, handed out advice, and served as the godfather of newborn babies. His word was law.

The second-largest structure on the hacienda was the stable. There were also workshops where tools were made, a mill for grinding corn, a storehouse piled high with dried meat and with the great stomachs of oxen filled with beef tallow, or fat, and a small church with its resident priest. Old carts with big wooden wheels stood in the patios, and burros waited sleepily by adobe walls, twitching their big ears to fend off flies.

A large room in the stable was set aside as a bunkhouse where unmarried vaqueros could curl up in their blankets at night. A man with a family might be allowed to build a simple hut on the outskirts of the main buildings, or he might rent such a place from the hacendado. Usually he had a small plot of land where he could grow corn, beans, and squash.

A hacienda might employ several hundred vaqueros. While the men now worked for wages, most of them were bound to their employer by debt. The nearest major town might be several days or weeks away by horseback or coach. There was only one place nearby to buy necessities and anything else—the hacienda store, which was stocked with goods like calico, buckskin, yellow leather shoes, knives, pottery, and religious objects. The ranch sold the vaquero goods on credit, or lent him money as an advance against wages, on condition that he work off what he owed.

Children inherited their parents' obligations, so a boy might already be in debt by the time he was old enough to join the work force. Later, the hacendado would lend him money to get married, to baptize his children, to celebrate religious festivals, and to bury his dead. A vaquero could go through life without ever seeing his wages. The few pesos he earned every month were simply credited to his account. Mexican workers were known as *peónes*, and this system, called debt peonage, existed all over Mexico until the early 1900s.

When the American artist Frederic Remington visited a hacienda in northern Mexico during the 1890s, he found that life for the vaqueros had scarcely changed for centuries. "They work for from eight to twelve dollars a month in Mexican coin," he wrote, "and live on the most simple diet imaginable. They are mostly *peóned,* or in hopeless debt to their *patróns*

Frederic Remington's drawing of a hacendado, or patrón, the owner of a hacienda. From Harper's Monthly, *December 1893.*

The administrator and his clerks recording peones' labor at Hacienda Peotillos, San Luis Potosí, Mexico.

[ranch owners], who go after any man who deserts the range and bring him back by force."

True, it was poorly paid work with plenty of risks, dangers, and hardships. But no one looked down on a vaquero on horseback. At home in the saddle, he had the dignity of a man who feels pride in his work and confidence in his ability to do a tough job well.

Without complaining, he worked in bad weather, tracked down stray animals, went without food, and slept on the ground. He was loyal to his ranch. And his hospitality knew no bounds. It was said that he would share his last tortilla with any stranger who happened by.

Mexican vaqueros and their families lived in simple dwellings like these.

Youngsters growing up on a hacienda were practically raised on a pony's back. One of a boy's earliest memories was the rhythm of a horse in motion. He never had to learn how to ride. And he played daily at roping from the time he was old enough to pick up a rope and throw it. His first targets were usually weathered mesquite fence posts. There were plenty of them, and they were just the right height. By the time a boy was six or seven, he had graduated to moving targets, such as chickens and rabbits.

A young fellow who had not yet mastered all the skills of a full-fledged vaquero was a *vaquerito*. To call a boy a good vaquerito was a compliment, but to call him a vaquero was the highest praise. It meant that he had earned his spurs.

Girls did not expect to become *vaqueras*. Back then, cowherding was considered strictly a man's job. Women ruled over their large families, delivered babies as midwives, tended the sick and injured, and prepared bodies for burial. Boys and girls knew from the very beginning what their life's work would be, and they began preparing for it almost as soon as they could walk.

"We would go out on the prairie and make a house," recalled Stella Guevara, who grew up as a vaquero's daughter. "This we did by drawing with a sharp stick a house outline in the dirt. . . . We made tortillas of mud and water. Then we made tamales from those large leaves and mud. . . . The boys would ride their stick horses off to be vaqueros."

Boys learned the skills they would need by tagging after and imitating their fathers. "My father taught me what I know," said Enemorio Serna. "I started going with him at age seven. I started breaking horses at eleven."

In California, the northernmost outpost of the Spanish empire, cattle ranching was introduced by missionaries led by Father Junípero Serra, who arrived with Spanish soldiers in 1769. The soldiers built *presidios,* or forts, along the Pacific Coast. Father Serra's priests established a chain of twenty-one missions, separated by a day's travel on horseback, extending from San Diego north to Sonoma.

As in Mexico two centuries earlier, the padres conscripted thousands of Indians to work as laborers on mission lands, which had been taken from the local tribes. They trained many of their young converts to rope and brand, ride herd and break horses. Cattle raising, dominated by the missions, became California's main industry.

Mission San Carlos Borromeo. Established by Franciscan missionaries at Monterey, California, it was moved to Carmel in 1771. Painting by Oriana Day, late nineteenth century.

Franciscan missionaries established twenty-one missions in California. Drawing by José Cisneros.

In 1821, Mexico declared its independence from Spain. California became part of the new Mexican Republic, along with Texas, present-day Utah and Nevada, and parts of present-day Arizona, New Mexico, Colorado, and Wyoming. Before long, the missionaries living in California, who were still loyal to Spain, were ordered by the Mexican government to return home. Their lands were snapped up by private owners, who recruited large numbers of Indian vaqueros from the disbanding missions.

Almost any Mexican citizen with Spanish blood could secure a grant of land on which to raise cattle. Holdings of forty thousand acres or more were common. California was so large, and the number of residents so small, that few landowners bothered to survey their property. The population in 1821 included 3,720 "Europeans"—anyone with Spanish blood—and some 30,000 mission Indians.

These vast California *ranchos* were very much like the haciendas that still flourished in Mexico. Indian vaqueros earned a small wage and became bound to their ranchos by debt. They lived in simple huts clustered near the main ranchhouse, the adobe *casa,* or in small villages, *rancherías,* scattered over the rancho. And they paid homage to their wealthy *ranchero.*

Roping a steer on a California rancho.

The government in Mexico was far away, and the ranchero, the owner of the ranch, was master of all he surveyed.

In California, roundups took place every spring. The vaquero drove his horse through milling seas of steers, separating his rancho's cattle from those of neighbors' herds and then branding new calves. After the roundup, at the mass cattle slaughters known as *matanzas,* he roped and tied one steer after another, killing each beast with a single flashing thrust of his long knife.

These early California vaqueros were rated as the best horsemen in the world by those who saw them in action. "The Indians who do this work are well acquainted with the manner of catching cattle," reported George Evans, an American who visited California in 1832. "You will see an Indian galloping swift as wind across the plains, and in a short time he has a steer singled out from the herd before him and the lasso thrown over his horns.

"The horse well understands his part of the tragedy. The moment he sees the well-directed rope fall over the head of the victim, he suddenly stops, and the next moment the beef is brought to his knees; as soon as he rises, he is led off to the place of slaughter. . . . I have seen some very good riders in Mexico, but these Californians are much better, and it is said that they will throw the lasso better with their feet than Mexicans can with the hand."

Working swiftly with their sharp knives, vaqueros stripped off the animal's hide right on the spot and staked it out to dry in the sun. They cut out the tallow, which was later boiled in huge vats until it liquefied. Then they cut the best meat into long strips, which were dipped in brine and hung to dry. The rest of the carcass was left to be scavenged by buzzards, coyotes, and grizzly bears. For years afterward, the killing grounds were littered with the bleached skulls and bones of cattle. They became known as *calaveras,* places of skulls.

The ranchos prospered by selling hides and tallow to Yankee trading ships that sailed up and down the California coast. Huge stacks of folded hides, called "California banknotes," and massive barrels of tallow were shipped around Cape Horn to Boston and other New England ports, where the hides were turned into all kinds of leather products and the tallow into candles and soap.

An Indian rancheria.

Californians Catching Wild Horses with Riata. *Painting by Hugo Wilhelm Arthur Nahl, mid-nineteenth century.*

CHAPTER FOUR

TOOLS OF THE TRADE

Over the centuries, ranching changed very little in New Spain. The most important tools for working cattle on the open range continued to be the vaquero's horse and his lariat.

He looked upon his lariat as his good right arm, and it was seldom out of reach of his nimble fingers. With it, he was ready for almost any task that came along.

He made his lariat himself, cutting long strips of untanned cowhide, which he soaked and stretched until they were pliable. Then he braided the leather strips into a rope, which he stretched again, oiled, and softened, working it over with loving care until he was satisfied that it was ready to use.

A typical lariat was about 60 feet long and as thick around as a man's little finger. There were longer ropes, *reatas largas,* which ran to 110 feet or more. Children had their own pint-size lariats. It seemed that everyone was always roping for practice, and that every target was fair game. Dogs, pigs, and chickens became as expert at dodging the rope as the vaqueros were at throwing it.

Coyotes were considered the toughest wild animals to rope, and a man who managed to snare one was greatly admired. While he took pride in his feat, he would say with modesty, *"Ese fue un supo,"* "That was a lucky throw."

Vaqueros also made fine horsehair ropes, *mecates*, which were used for reins and halters. Different colors of hair were blended together, forming ropes that were not only strong but beautiful.

The hair was cut from the tails and manes of the ranch's herd of mares, horses kept for breeding. The tails and manes of stallions, the riding horses, were never cut. "The mares would take a dislike to the stallions if we cut their tails," an old vaquero explained. "They would lose their respect and affection for them, and would not recognize them as their stallions." Vaqueros expressed a strong sense of machismo, a belief in masculine dominance and superiority, even when it came to their horses.

In the early days, vaqueros made their own saddles as well. They took as a model the old Spanish war saddle on which the conquistadores had ridden into Mexico, and they gradually transformed it to meet the special needs of cowhands working in cattle country.

They added a large round-topped saddle horn as a sturdy anchor to which their lariats could be secured when they roped a steer. They made the saddle's stirrup straps longer, allowing the rider to get a better knee grip. The stirrups themselves were carved out of wood. They were big enough to let a man stand upright while riding down a steep slope or trotting along the trail.

Saddles became stronger and more compact. At first, vaqueros placed a blanket, a piece of leather, or an animal skin over the seat of the saddle to provide a little comfort. Later they devised the *mochila,* a removable leather covering that fit snugly over the entire saddle and often had built-in saddlebags.

Vaqueros working in brush country covered their stirrups with leather casings called *tapaderas,* or taps, which shielded the rider's feet from cactus thorns. In the deserts of northwestern Mexico, saddles were rigged with *armas,* huge slabs of cowhide that hung down from the saddle on either side, covering and protecting the rider's thighs and lower legs.

A Mexican vaquero wearing protective armas. Photographed around 1900 in Berino, New Mexico.

Later, vaqueros attached smaller, lightweight *armitas* directly to their legs. These in turn developed into seatless leather leggings called *chaparreras,* or chaps, for protection while riding through mesquite and chaparral thickets. Chaps also protected a rider against rope burns, abrasions from trees and corral posts, and horse bites. They were made of smooth buckskin, or of goat, sheep, wolf, bear, or lion pelts with the wool or fur left on the outside of the chaps.

Since the vaquero often spent his days from sunrise to sunset in the saddle, no single piece of equipment was more important. A well-made saddle, lovingly maintained, was important to his horse, too. A rider with a gentle hand and a good rig could travel for hours and still have a healthy horse, but a poorly made saddle could make a horse sore in no time at all.

A Mexican saddle with a large saddle horn and big wooden stirrups.

As a rule, the saddle was the vaquero's personal property, while the horses he rode belonged to the ranch. Each morning he selected a mount from the ranch's herd of saddle horses, called the *remuda,* from the Spanish word *remudar,* "to exchange." Each man had a string of favorite horses in the remuda, so he could change mounts during the day.

Many of these animals had been captured out on the plains, where they roamed freely until they were at least three years old. They were called *mesteños,* stray animals, a Spanish word that American cowboys later twisted into "mustang."

When the time came to tame a wild mustang, vaqueros would rope the horse by his front legs, throw him to the ground, and place a halter on his head. The mustang was then tied by a long rope to a fence post or tree and allowed to fight it out. He would pull back, jump forward, get a front foot over the rope, fall over, and squeal with rage, all the while struggling to get free.

He might fight the rope for two days or more without being fed before he finally began to calm down. By then, his neck was so sore from the rope that nothing could make him pull back. His hind legs were sore too. Vaqueros could now "sideline" the horse, tying a hind foot to his shoulder. When a horse submitted to this indignity without fighting back, he was partly broken and ready for his first saddle.

At first, he was ridden once or twice a day until he could be handled easily. After that, he was trained for use in rounding up stock, cutting out steers from the rest of the herd, and roping. He learned to perform nimble cuts and turns to head off any calf trying to hightail it back to the brush. In time, he was given a name, usually one that indicated his color (El Mojino, The Dark Brown) or his temperament (El Cohete, The Skyrocket).

"You gave the horse who knew the most to a young kid, so he could

learn from the horse," vaquero Martín Mendietta recalled. "He just had to stay on, and the horse would do the work."

Each vaquero had his favorite horses, which he used exclusively. He believed that through long association, a good horse learned every mood and quirk of his rider, could read his rider's mind, and from the rider's movements would anticipate his slightest wish.

Only stallions were considered suitable for riding. Like their Spanish overseers, vaqueros refused to ride mares. Mares were kept for breeding. A man felt humiliated if he had to ride a mare.

In the early days, the vaquero wore any clothes he happened to own, but as the years passed, he developed a distinct and practical way of dressing. While his clothing varied from one region to the next, according to the terrain he rode, and changed in appearance over the years, it always singled him out as a working cowhand.

Breaking a mustang. One of many scenes depicted by Frederic Remington after his visit to a cattle-raising hacienda near Chihuahua, Mexico, in 1893.

Mounting a Wild One. *Drawing by Frederic Remington. From* Harper's Monthly, *March 1894.*

To shield his head and eyes from the Mexican sun, he wore a *sombrero,* from the word *sombrear,* "to shade"—a wide-brimmed hat made of straw, leather, or felt. Held in place with a *barbiquejo,* a chin strap, it often was decorated with a colorful band. A sombrero might have a low flat crown with a straight stiff brim, or a tall crown, several inches high, with a soft floppy brim. Whatever its shape, it was always impressively large, with a brim wide enough to shade the wearer's face. Because of its practicality, the big wide-brimmed hat became a familiar cowboy trademark.

Under his sombrero, the vaquero wore a kerchief tied over his head. His hair was parted in the middle and brushed back into a long braid that might hang down his back, or be folded up and tucked under his hat.

A vaquero usually carried a brightly colored *sarape,* or poncho, which was thrown over his shoulder like a shawl or carried on the back of his saddle. A sarape offered protection when it rained and warmth when it was cold. It served as a bed at night when the vaquero slept under the stars. Waved wildly in the air, it was used to haze cattle during roundups and stampedes.

Over the years, the vaquero's clothing became more decorative, with little flourishes and embellishments. The lowliest peón took pride in his appearance and in the trappings of his horse, copying the elaborate gear of his wealthy hacendado or ranchero as far as he was able.

In Mexico's northern provinces and in Spanish California, he wore a short-waisted *chaqueta,* or jacket, made of leather or cloth—the forerunner of the short denim jacket that would become so popular among American cowboys. The vaquero's jacket was often trimmed with bright embroidery or braid and with fancy buttons along the sides and on the pocket flaps.

A red *faja,* or sash, was wrapped several times around his waist. His tight-fitting pants buttoned down the sides and were tucked into leather *botas,* or leggings, which covered his

A vaquero waves his sarape to haze cattle. Drawing by Frederic Remington. From Harper's Monthly, *March 1894.*

lower legs down to the ankles. The garter around his right leg held a scabbard containing his indispensable long knife.

His shoes might be simple leather *huaraches,* or sandals; almost any kind of flat-heeled buckskin or leather shoes; or perhaps leather boots, probably hand-me-downs from some Spaniard. High-heeled cowboy boots, as we know them today, were still far in the future. In warmer climates, many vaqueros continued to go barefoot.

Whatever his footgear, the vaquero always had a pair of heavy iron *espuelas,* or spurs, strapped to his boots or to the ankles of his bare feet. Spurs were a proud emblem of his calling. They jingled and jangled when he walked, announcing his presence. But he never walked when he could ride.

He spent so much time in the saddle, he developed a bowlegged gait, walking as though he were lame whenever he found himself on the ground. Ambling along, he listed from side to side, like a ship in heavy seas. But let him get his feet in the stirrups, and he went loping over the plains with an easy grace, clinging to his horse like bark to a tree.

The tall, wide-brimmed sombrero, the leather leggings, and the short, trim jacket identify this man as a vaquero from northern Mexico. Though he is shown with a revolver in Frederic Remington's drawing, many vaqueros considered firearms unmanly and never carried them. From Harper's Monthly, *December 1893.*

*Cheered on by spectators, two vaqueros race their horses to the finish line.
Painting by Ernest Narjot, mid-nineteenth century.*

◆◆◆◆◆◆◆◆◆◆◆◆◆◆◆◆◆◆◆◆◆◆◆◆

CHAPTER FIVE

CONTESTS AND GAMES

Since the vaquero practically lived in the saddle, it's not surprising that his favorite pastimes were tests of horsemanship. He was always ready to place a bet, take up a dare, or join in a competitive and often dangerous game.

One popular stunt was to lean down from the side of a horse at full gallop and pluck from the ground a coin, an arrow, a kerchief, or, in a gruesome sport called *carrera del gallo,* a live rooster buried in sand with only its head showing. If the rider swung back into the saddle waving the wing-flapping rooster in his hand, he won all bets along with whoops of approval from the crowd.

Holidays and celebrations featured horseraces of every imaginable kind. *La sortija,* the ring race, required a sharp eye and split-second timing. Vaqueros armed with short wooden lances raced at a gallop toward a tiny golden ring hanging from a slender thread. The rider who managed to skewer the ring with his lance won it as a prize. He could then present it as a gift to a young woman he wanted to impress.

Another test of horsemanship involved two silver coins. The rider placed one coin between each knee and the side of the saddle. Then he galloped around an obstacle course, jumping hurdles and weaving around obstacles. The idea was to stay so firmly in the saddle that, at the end of the course, the two coins were still in place.

In an emergency, a man's life might depend on his ability to bring his horse to a sudden stop—during a stampede, perhaps, or to avoid a sinkhole, a rattlesnake, or the edge of a cliff. This critical skill was displayed in a contest called *rayar*, to draw a line. Starting from opposite directions, two riders galloped toward a line drawn in the dirt. As they approached the line, they pulled back on the reins. Their horses were trained to drop onto their haunches and skid to a stop. The rider whose horse stopped closest to the *raya*, the line, was the winner.

Colear, tailing the bull, was both a sport and a practical working skill. The *coleador*, the tailer, galloped up behind a bull, reached out from the right to grab its tail, passed the tail under his right leg, twisted it around his saddle horn, then wheeled his horse sharply to the left, throwing the bull off balance and causing the stunned animal to crash headlong to the ground.

Tailing a bull required a certain knack. With the right leverage and timing, a small man on a horse could topple even the biggest bull. The reputation of being the best coleador in the district guaranteed a vaquero the respect of his *compadres*, or comrades, and the admiration of numerous young women.

When a man really wanted to show off, he took part in the *paso de la muerte*, the ride of death. In one version of this risky sport, a vaquero on horseback galloped alongside a wild horse—a *bronco*, from the Spanish word for "rough." He jumped from his mount onto the animal's back and rode that bucking bronco until he was thrown, or until the exhausted ani-

Tailing bulls was both a practical working technique and a popular sport, requiring courage, skill, and perfect timing. From Harper's Monthly, *March 1894.*

mal was tamed. Or he might pit his strength against a wild bull, roping the animal, then leaping onto its back and riding the enraged beast as he clung tightly to the rope.

There were usually no doctors around to mend bruises, sprains, and broken bones. An injured man would be tended by a *curandera,* a woman wise in the ways of folk medicine.

No sport was more dangerous than the grizzly bear hunts carried out by Indian vaqueros in California. Grizzlies, powerful giants with five-inch claws in each mighty paw, roamed the California coast country. When a bear was sighted, four or five men working together lassoed the beast by its

legs and throat and choked off its air. As the dazed grizzly was being led away, the vaqueros took turns riding up close to the animal and provoking it to charge.

Captured grizzlies were pitted in violent battles against wild bulls. These fights were staged at arenas built especially for the purpose at Spanish missions, presidios, and *pueblos,* or towns, and they attracted enthusiastic crowds. The opponents were tied to each other with a long rope: One end was tied to the bear's hind leg, the other to the bull's fore-leg. A grizzly sometimes killed several bulls before it was mortally gored.

Back at the ranch, in the cool of the evening, vaqueros had a chance to relax around the campfire, swapping tales and exchanging jokes with com-

Roping a Wild Grizzly. *Painting by James Walker, ca. 1877. Captured bears were pitted in battle against wild bulls.*

padres who understood what a vaquero's life was like. Sometimes they told haunting stories about spirits and ghosts, and about men and women with magical powers far beyond a poor mortal's ken.

Writer Arnold Rojas, who called himself "The Last of the Vaqueros," passed along the story of *El Güero Rosalio*, Blond Rosalio, a legendary vaquero who could throw a bull simply by lifting its tail. He caught fish with his bare hands. And he roped cattle while riding a wild horse without saddle or bridle.

Rosalio never slept in a house. He built a platform in a tree and slept there. He disappeared for days at a time, turning himself into a coyote and running with the pack. No one dared shoot at the coyotes seen on the ranch, for fear that one of them might be Rosalio.

Swapping tales around the campfire. Drawing by Frederic Remington. From Harper's Monthly, *February 1894.*

When he died, they laid him out on a rawhide bed in a small house on the ranch. As soon as everyone had left, the house caught fire and burned to the ground. But the bed on which Rosalio's body lay wasn't even scorched. The blanket that covered the bed had no ashes on it. And Rosalio's body was gone. "It had been spirited away from under our very noses," Rojas wrote. "We never found a trace of it again."

While vaqueros were imaginative storytellers, few of the men could read or even write their names. Many of them played musical instruments, however, and it was a pitiful hacienda that did not have a string band to strum away at fiestas, weddings, and dances. These were community events, attended by everyone on the ranch.

A vaquero dance band. Drawing by Frederic Remington. From Harper's Monthly, *December 1893.*

Women arrived wearing gay shawls and bright billowing dresses, and the men whooped and stomped their feet and whirled their partners, raising the dust from the dirt dance floor. Old folks gossiped on the sidelines, children chased each other through the crowd, babies dozed in their mothers' arms, and the hacendado held court, bestowing favors on one and all.

Everyone knew the words to traditional Mexican *corridos,* or ballads, and they vied with each other to make up new lyrics of their own. They sang about the pain of love, the daring deeds of outlaw heroes, the courage of a fierce bull, the virtues of a favorite horse. "Mi Caballo Bayo" pays tribute to a vaquero who grieves for his beloved bay-colored horse:

> *He won't be coming back to his stable anymore,*
> *My loyal horse, he won't be coming back, no!*
> *He won't be neighing with joy anymore,*
> *As he did when I caressed him.*
>
> *Cursed be the bad luck*
> *That suddenly took him away, oh!*
> *My poor bay horse,*
> *How I cried when he was no more.*

At the Battle of the Alamo on March 6, 1836, the entire garrison of Texans, besieged by the Mexican army, was wiped out. Six weeks later, Texans defeated the Mexicans at San Jacinto, crying, "Remember the Alamo!" and Mexico was compelled to recognize the independence of Texas. Painting by Frederick Coffay Yohn.

◆◆◆◆◆◆◆◆◆◆◆◆◆◆◆◆◆◆◆◆◆◆◆◆◆◆

VAQUEROS, BUCKAROOS, AND COWBOYS

For generations, the vaquero practiced his trade with tools and skills handed down from father to son. On the sprawling haciendas of Mexico and Texas, and the sun-drenched ranchos of Spanish California, the days passed slowly. Time seemed to stand still. It wasn't until the early 1800s, when Mexico broke away from Spain, that the vaquero's world finally began to change.

Adventurous settlers from the United States, men and women known to their Spanish-speaking neighbors as Anglos because they spoke English, were trickling into Texas, New Mexico, Arizona, and California—a vast region that was now part of the independent Mexican Republic. Before long, Anglos outnumbered the Mexicans in Texas. In 1836, the Texans declared their own independence, and in 1845, Texas joined the Union as the twenty-eighth state.

Soon afterward, Mexico and the United States went to war in a dispute over territory that each country claimed. U.S. troops fought their way to

Mexico City, where, on September 14, 1847, the American flag was raised over a foreign capital for the first time. Defeated, Mexico signed over to the United States a huge block of territory: all of present-day California, Nevada, and Utah, and parts of Arizona, New Mexico, Colorado, and Wyoming. Mexico also agreed that the Río Bravo, which is known in the United States as the Rio Grande, would be the international boundary of Texas.

By the time the peace treaty was signed, gold had been discovered at Sutter's Creek in California. Suddenly, there was a pressing demand for beef on the hoof. To feed the hordes of hungry miners pouring into the newly opened gold fields around San Francisco, ranchers in southern California began to drive their cattle north.

During the 1850s, Indian vaqueros herded thousands of cattle over rugged mountain passes, through the untamed San Joaquin Valley, and along California's wild Pacific coast. The men were a colorful sight, their bright-red sashes flapping in the wind as they guided the slow-moving

Texas remained an independent republic under its Lone Star flag for almost ten years before being admitted to the Union in 1845.

California vaqueros driving livestock past the mission of San Gabriel.

herds. Vaqueros patrolled long lines of swaying backs, tramping hoofs, and clashing horns—the cattle bawling and complaining, the horses snorting and neighing, the rawhide on saddles creaking with every step the horses took.

Herds of elk, antelope, and deer watched from a distance. Cattle panicked and stampeded during thunderstorms at night. Bands of outlaws and hostile Ute and Mohave Indians rode out of the darkness to raid the herds and skirmish with the vaqueros. Those were the first great cattle drives to take place in the American West.

When the gold rush ended, cattle raising in California began a slow decline as ranches gradually gave way to farms. But on the sparsely settled Texas prairie, cattle were multiplying faster than anyone could count. These animals had descended from herds left behind by missionaries who had gone back to Spain, and from herds abandoned by Mexican ranch owners who had fled south across the Rio Grande when Texas broke away from Mexico, leaving both their cattle and their vaqueros behind.

Texas cattle were not at all like the tame and docile animals that Anglo settlers in Texas were accustomed to raising back East. These cattle were as wild as buffalo or antelope, and now millions of them were wandering

The Stampede.
Painting by Frederic Remington, 1908.

around loose. They clustered together in bunches, hiding in thickets by day and running by night. They could go days without water. Their sense of smell was keener than a deer's. And they had long, sharp, dangerous horns.

If a man tried to approach on foot, a bull would paw the earth, toss his head in anger, lower his horns, and charge. The animals could be approached only on horseback. And even then, bulls often tried to attack both man and horse.

American settlers considered the wild cattle they found in Texas fair game, free for the taking. Yet they had little idea how to manage large numbers of fierce, far-ranging longhorns. Most of the early Texas settlers were farmers who raised a few cattle on the side. They had never practiced large-

A Texas longhorn.

scale ranching, as the Spaniards and Mexicans had on their ranchos and haciendas.

Handling wild cattle on the open range was new to the Americans but centuries old to the Mexican vaqueros. And so the Americans turned to the vaqueros for help. "They are universally acknowledged to be best hands that can be [found] for the management of cattle, horses, and other livestock," a Texas settler reported.

Mexican vaqueros still living in Texas began to capture mustangs for the newcomers and round up wild steers. As the Americans watched the vaqueros work, they too became skilled at taming mustangs and roping steers.

Guarding the herd.

In this way, the North American cowboy learned his trade from the Mexican vaquero. He learned how to break a bronco, ride herd, throw a lariat, and use a branding iron. He adopted the vaquero's saddle, with its big saddle horn designed for roping, and his clothing, which shielded him from the sun's hot glare and protected him against all the thorns that stick and sting. And he borrowed many of the vaquero's Spanish words, very often changing their pronunciations but keeping their meanings as he made them part of his own workaday vocabulary—words like rodeo, lariat, lasso, chaps, mustang, and bronco.

The word "vaquero," as pronounced by American cowboys, became "bukera," and finally "buckaroo." And for a time, anyone working cattle, whether in Texas, California, or elsewhere, was known as a buckaroo. It wasn't until the late 1860s, when the Texans began to drive their cattle north to the new railroads in Kansas, that the term "cowboy" came into widespread use.

Going home. Painting by Edward Borein, ca. 1915.

CHAPTER SEVEN

THE LAST OF THE VAQUEROS

At first, there wasn't much demand for Texas longhorns. Texas still had more cattle than people, and the herds were increasing faster than any local need for beef.

The animals could not be driven to the crowded cities of the East because of the great distances. And fresh meat couldn't be shipped far because there was no ice or refrigeration to preserve it. Cattle were valued mainly for their hides and tallow, which were sent by pack horse or ox cart to the nearby Gulf coast and loaded aboard steamers bound for New Orleans and to the eastern seaboard. Like Spanish and Mexican ranchers before them, Texans stripped the cattle of their hides, rendered the fat, and left most of the meat for coyotes and wolves.

Oddly enough, it was the coming of the railroad that ushered in the great cattle drives of the late 1800s and the golden age of the American cowboy. By the time the American Civil War ended in 1865, the iron horse had pushed its path halfway across the continent. Large herds of cattle could now be driven north a thousand miles from Texas to railroad towns in Kansas, where the animals were loaded aboard freight cars and shipped to meat-packing plants in Kansas City and Chicago.

As the demand for fresh beef grew, cattle ranches began to spring up all across the northern plains, stocked with animals brought up the trail from Texas. Soon a vast tract of cattle country stretched from Colorado up through Wyoming, Montana, and the Dakotas. And wherever these new ranches appeared, they relied on the hard-won skills of the young men who were beginning to call themselves cowboys.

Cowboys came from many backgrounds and from all parts of the country. Some were discharged soldiers, back from the Civil War, who went

Texas cattle crossing a stream. This drawing appeared in Harper's Weekly, *October 19, 1867—the year in which the first big cattle drives from Texas to Kansas took place.*

A herd of Texas longhorns being driven to the cattle rendezvous at Dodge City, Kansas. From Frank Leslie's Illustrated Newspaper, *July 27, 1878.*

west looking for a fresh start or in search of adventure. Others were newly freed slaves, black men from Texas and other southern states who found work as professional cowhands. Mexican cowhands, who continued to call themselves vaqueros, made up more than half the workforce on most Texas and southwestern ranches, and were hired by ranches throughout the West and Northwest.

Whatever their backgrounds, these men were united by the conviction that a man without a horse is helpless. They had to be superb riders, skilled with the lariat. And yet black and Mexican cowhands faced prejudice and discrimination wherever they happened to work.

One outfit in Texas paid its Anglo hands a wage of $20 to $25 a month but reduced that to $10 or $12 a month for vaqueros, even when they were recognized as outstanding ropers and bronco busters. And vaqueros seldom rose above cowboy ranks to become foremen or trail bosses. At the huge King Ranch in Texas, most of the ranch hands were Mexican-American vaqueros, while all of the foremen were Anglos.

The heyday of the American cowboy lasted only a few decades. A network of railroad tracks was spreading throughout the West, and when the railroads reached Texas, long trail drives were no longer necessary. Meanwhile, barbed wire, invented in 1874, had made it possible to fence off large areas cheaply and easily. And as cattle ranchers and farmers put up long stretches of barbed-wire fence, they put an end to the open range.

By the 1890s, the open-range roundup and the long trail drive had passed into history, and the cowboy's way of life had changed forever. Cattle no longer wandered freely across the prairies. Instead, the animals were confined to fenced pastures dotted with windmills and cattle guards,

The Ascarate ranch in the state of Chihuahua, Mexico, around 1900.

where ranchers could keep each breed separate and control what the animals ate. Roundups, which once had ranged over hundreds of square miles, now were conducted inside barbed-wire enclosures. Men on horseback still drove cattle, but only from fenced pastures to railroad loading pens a few miles away. The rodeo became a spectator sport, a stylized performance to which admission was charged.

In Mexico, political turmoil had turned many of the great cattle-raising haciendas into desolate battlefields. During the violent revolution that shook the nation from 1910 to 1920, ranchers lost their herds and vaqueros their livelihoods as opposing armies swept back and forth across the countryside. When the fighting ended, the Mexican livestock industry began a slow recovery. By then, the old ways were dying out, as they already had in the United States.

Fences increased and pastures grew smaller, reducing the need for working cowhands. Vaqueros drove across the Mexican plains in pickup trucks instead of on horseback, and on the larger haciendas they even helped herd cattle at the controls of helicopters. In parts of Mexico, the

A Mexican-American vaquero.

old-time vaquero still rode the range as he had for hundreds of years, but modern ranching methods were fast elbowing him aside. He began to seem like a man out of the past, a link to a bygone era that will never come again.

Born to the saddle, he had always worked cattle much as his father, grandfather, great-grandfather, and even great-great-grandfather had done. And yet the Spanish, and later the Mexicans, had never glorified the figure of the vaquero in the same way that North Americans came to romanticize

Mexican Cowboys Coming to the Rodeo. *Painting by Frederic Remington, 1893.*

the image of the cowboy. No matter how skilled the vaquero was, how courageous, colorful, or proud, he continued to be regarded as just a poor laborer on horseback—a peón.

Even so, his legacy endures. Today, wherever a man chooses to call himself a cowboy, whenever he puts on a wide-brimmed hat, pulls on a pair of chaps, swings a lariat, brands a calf, rides a bucking bronco, or strums a guitar and sings a love song to his favorite horse, he is paying tribute to those barefoot Indian cowherders who started it all nearly five hundred years ago.

◆◆◆◆◆◆◆◆◆◆◆◆◆◆◆◆◆◆◆◆◆◆◆◆◆◆◆◆◆◆◆◆

My horse, my horse
Goes galloping.
My horse, my horse
Goes on and on.

On the wings of happiness,
My horse races on.
And in the arms of sorrow,
He carries me as well.

—From "Mi Caballo Blanco,"
a Chilean ballad

BIBLIOGRAPHY

◆◆◆◆◆◆◆◆◆◆◆◆◆◆◆◆◆◆◆◆◆◆◆◆◆◆

The Mexican vaquero has not fared nearly as well in literature, art, or history as his U.S. counterpart, the American cowboy. Unlike the cowboy, the vaquero was never exalted as a culture hero. A landless peón shackled by the system of debt peonage, he lacked the cowboy's freewheeling independence and mobility.

As Richard W. Slatta has noted, the legendary U.S. cowboy is closely associated in the national consciousness with the imagery of the frontier. Mexico never developed a version of the frontier myth, looking instead to the pre-Columbian Aztec past as a source of the Mexican national type.

Because the vaquero did not emerge as an important national icon, he has been the subject of few substantial, well-documented studies, and he remains a marginal figure in Mexican literature and film. The aristocratic Mexican charro, decked out in his elaborate silver-encrusted costume, has received far more attention than the humble vaquero, the true working cowhand, and the two are often mixed and confused.

For my account, I am particularly indebted to two outstanding scholarly works: *Cowboys of the Americas* by Richard W. Slatta (New Haven, Conn.: Yale

University Press, 1990) presents a sweeping panoramic history of the cowboy's rise and fall, from the Argentine pampas to the Canadian prairies; *Cowboy Culture: A Saga of Five Centuries* by David Dary (New York: Alfred A. Knopf, 1981) covers the same five-hundred-year period but focuses primarily on the working cowboy of North America.

Among other works that I found helpful:

Man on Horseback by Glenn R. Vernam (New York: Harper & Row, 1964) has an informative chapter on vaquero clothing and equipment through the centuries. *The Vaquero* by Arnold R. Rojas (Charlotte, N.C.: McNally and Loftin, 1964) and *Californios* by Jo Mora (Garden City, N.Y.: Doubleday & Company, 1949) are popular anecdotal works that explore the lives and traditions of California vaqueros. *Riders Across the Centuries: Horsemen of the Spanish Borderlands* (El Paso, Tex.: Texas Western Press, 1984) and *Riders of the Border* (El Paso, Tex.: Texas Western Press, 1971), both by José Cisneros, offer detailed drawings and brief descriptions of soldiers, missionaries, colonists, and vaqueros from the Spanish conquest to recent times. *Pony Tracks* by Frederic Remington (Norman, Okla.: University of Oklahoma Press, 1961; first published in 1895) includes a classic account, accompanied by drawings, of Remington's visit to a cattle-raising hacienda.

Vaquero: Genesis of the Texas Cowboy by William D. Wittliff (San Antonio, Tex.: Institute of Texas Cultures, 1972) is a photo essay about vaqueros working cattle in Mexico during the 1970s. And *Voices from the Wild Horse Desert: The Vaquero Families of the King and Kenedy Ranches* by Jane Clements Monday and Betty Bailey Colley (Austin, Tex.: University of Texas Press, 1997) is an account of vaquero families who have lived and worked in South Texas for six generations.

I also consulted the following histories: *Many Mexicos* by Lesley Byrd Simpson (Berkeley, Calif.: University of California Press, Fourth Revised Edition, 1966); *Triumphs and Tragedy: A History of the Mexican People* by Ramón Eduardo Ruiz (New York: W. W. Norton, 1992); and *Mexico: A History* by Robert Ryal Miller (Norman, Okla.: University of Oklahoma Press, 1985).

GLOSSARY

◆◆◆◆◆◆◆◆◆◆◆◆◆◆◆◆◆◆◆◆

Some sounds in Spanish have no direct equivalent in English; the pronunciation guide is an approximation.

armas (AHR mas) Stiff leather skirts that hang from each side of a Mexican saddle to protect the rider's legs.

armitas (ahr MEE tas) Smaller, lightweight armas that are attached directly to the rider's legs.

barbiquejo (bahr bih KEH ho) A sombrero chin strap.

botas (BOH tas) Leather boots or leggings.

bronco (BRONG koh) A wild, unbroken horse.

calaveras (kah lah VEH ras) Skulls, or places of skulls.

carrera del gallo (kahr REH ra del GUY yo) A rooster race.

casa (KAH sa) A house.

chaparreras (chah pahr REH ras) Leather chaps worn by ranch hands over ordinary trousers to protect the legs.

charro (CHAR roh) A gentleman rider.

chaqueta (chah KEH ta) A jacket.

coleador (kol leh ah DOHR) A horseman who practices the sport of tailing a bull.

colear (koh leh AR) To throw a running bull to the ground by twisting its tail.

compadre (kom PAH dreh) Mate, pal, or comrade.

conquistador (kon kee sta DOHR) A fifteeth-century Spanish soldier who defeated the Indian civilizations of Mexico, Central America, and Peru; a conqueror.

corrido (kohr REE doh) A Mexican folksong.

curandera (koo rahn DEH ra) A woman wise in the ways of healing.

dar la vuelta (dahr la VWEHL ta) To wrap the end of the rope around the saddle horn when roping a cow; anglicized to "dally."

desjarretadera (dess hahr reh ta DEH ra) A hocking knife used in colonial Spanish America to disable and capture running cattle.

encomendero (en koh men DEH ro) The holder of an encomienda.

encomienda (en kohm YEN da) A royal land grant, including Indian inhabitants, made to Spanish conquerers.

espuelas (ess PWEH las) Spurs.

faja (FAH ha) A sash worn around the waist.

garrocha (gahr ROH cha) A long iron-tipped pole used to prod cattle in Spanish America.

hacendado (ah sen DAH doh) The landowner or proprietor of a hacienda.

hacienda (ahs YEN da) A large estate, often raising livestock.

huaraches (wa RAH ches) Sandals.

lazo (LAH soh) A long rope with a running noose at one end, used to catch horses and cattle; anglicized to "lasso."

mangana (mahn GAH na) An overhand rope throw that catches the animals front legs as it steps into the noose; from *mano* for "hand" or "forefoot."

matanza (mah TAHN sa) The organized slaughter of cattle for their hides and tallow.

mecate (meh CAH teh) A finely woven horsehair rope.

mesteño (mes TEH nyo) A wild horse; anglicized to "mustang."

mestizo (mes TEE soh) A person of mixed Spanish and Native American ancestry.

mochila (moh CHEE la) A leather saddle covering, often with built-in saddlebags.

padre (PAH dreh) Father; a Catholic priest.

paso de la muerte (PAH so deh la MWER teh) A bareback ride on a wild horse or bull.

patrón (pah TRAWN) A ranch owner or boss.

peón (peh AWN) A manual laborer or farmworker, usually landless.

piale (pee AH leh) An underhand rope throw that catches the animal's hind legs; from *pie* for foot.

presidio (preh SEE deeoh) A Spanish fort.

pueblo (PWEB loh) A village or town.

ranchería (rahn cheh REE ah) A small Indian village on a rancho.

ranchero (rahn CHEH roh) The owner of a rancho.

rancho (RAHN choh) A farm or ranch, especially a cattle ranch in Spanish California or a modest ranch in Mexico.

rayar (rah YAR) A horse-stopping contest.

reata (reh AH ta) A rawhide rope; "la reata," the rope, anglicized to "lariat."

remuda (reh MOO da) A herd of saddle horses from which ranch hands select their mounts.

rodeo (ro DEH oh) A roundup of cattle, usually for branding.

sarape (sah RAH peh) A long blanket-like shawl, worn especially in Mexico.

sombrero (sohm BREH roh) A wide-brimmed Mexican hat.

sortija (sohr TEE ha) A ring race.

tapaderas (tah pah DEH ras) Leather coverings that hang from each side of a Mexican saddle to cover the rider's legs.

vaquerito (vah keh REE toh) A young and unseasoned vaquero.

vaquero (vah KEH roh) A cowboy or ranch hand.

ACKNOWLEDGMENTS AND PICTURE CREDITS

◆◆◆◆◆◆◆◆◆◆◆◆◆◆◆◆◆◆◆◆◆◆◆◆◆◆◆◆◆◆◆◆◆◆◆

Special thanks to Darwin Bahm for his generous assistance in finding illustrations for this book, to Patricia Wong of the Oakland Public Library for her suggestions, and to the following:

Jerry Bloomer, the R. W. Norton Art Gallery; Dennis Daily, Rio Grande Historical Collection, New Mexico State University Library; Ellen Harding, the California State Library; Harvey Jones, the Oakland Museum of California; Marlene R. Miller, the Arlington Gallery, Santa Barbara; Alison Poulsen, the Autry Museum of Western Heritage; Scott Shields, the California Historical Society.

Thanks also to Charles J. Arnold and Phil Gerrard for aiding and abetting my field research in California.

My gratitude to Liora Mondlak for her translations of vaquero corridos, to Lucia Gonzalez for additional help with the corridos, and to Viki Ortiz for her advice and recommendations concerning Spanish language, terminology, and pronunciation.

INDEX

◆◆◆◆◆◆◆◆◆◆◆◆◆

Page numbers in **bold** type refer to illustrations.